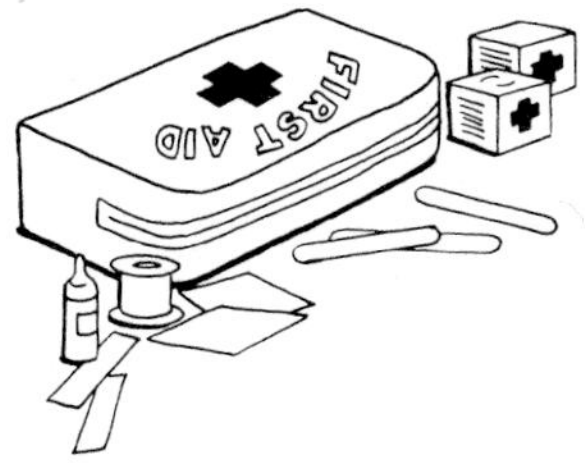
FIRST AID

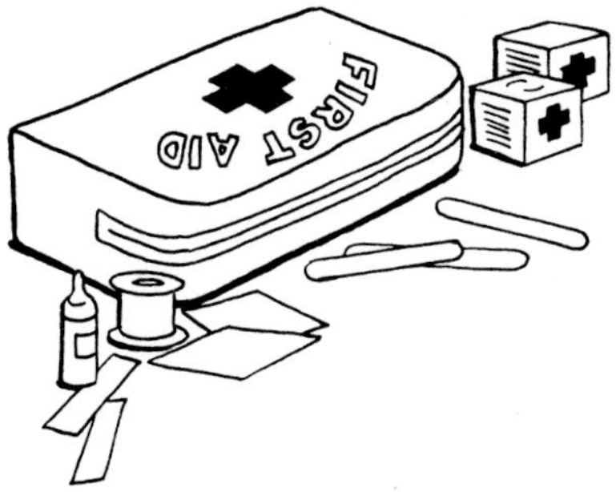
FIRST AID

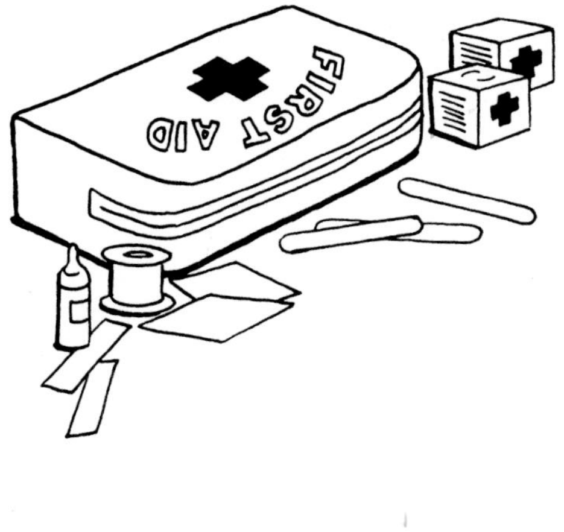
FIRST AID

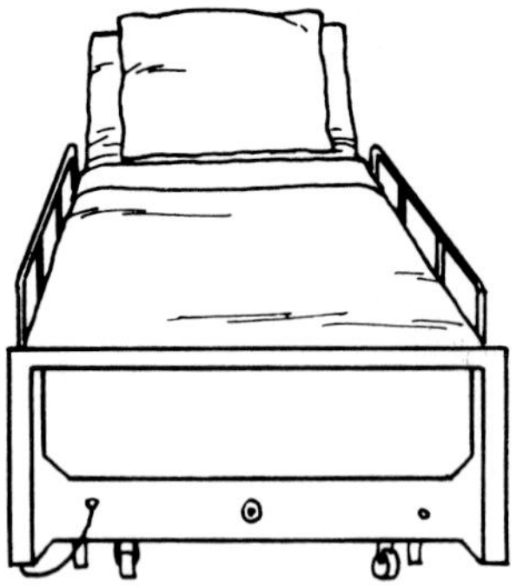
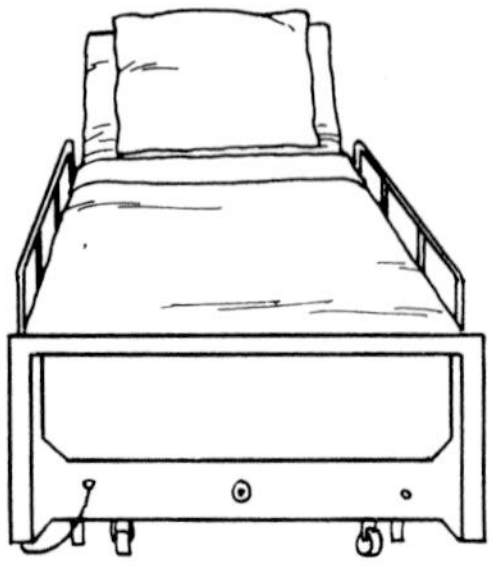
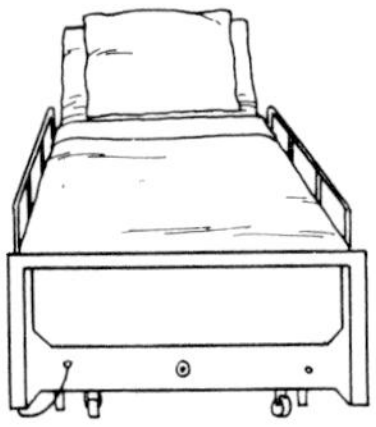
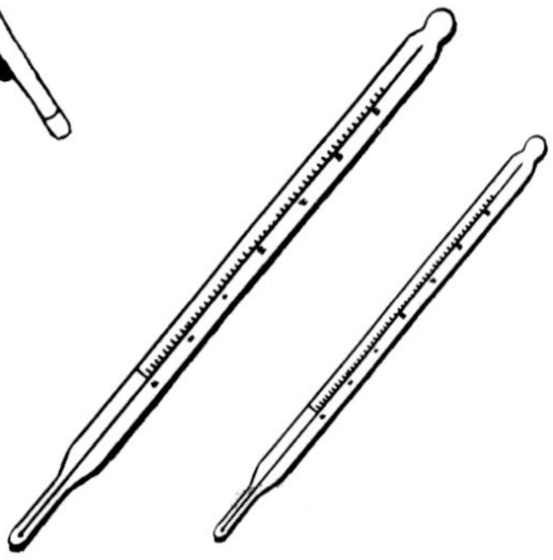

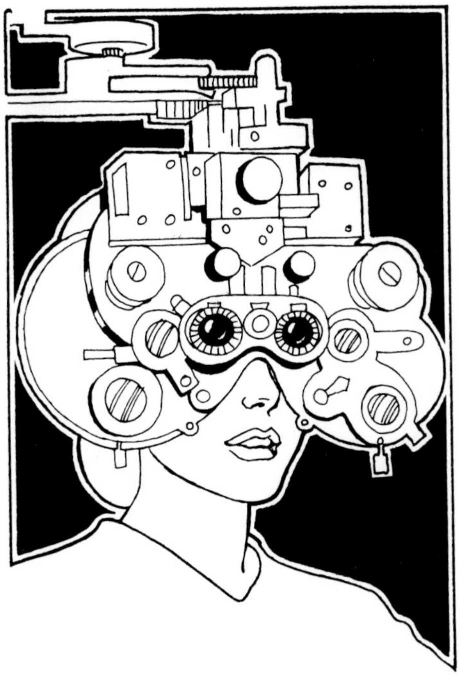

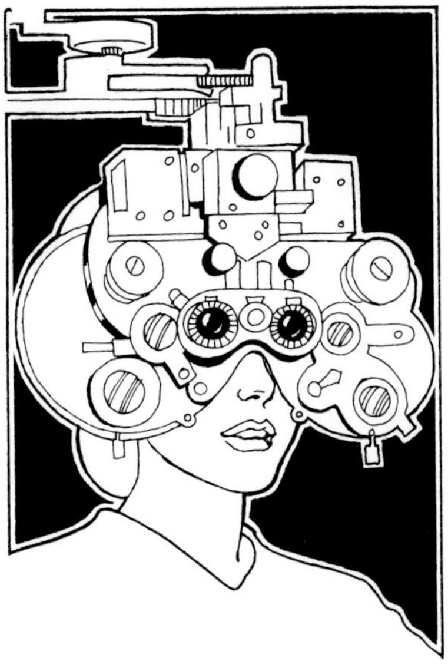

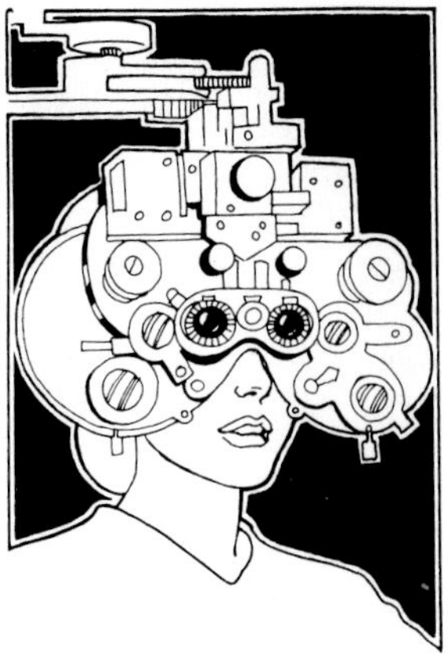

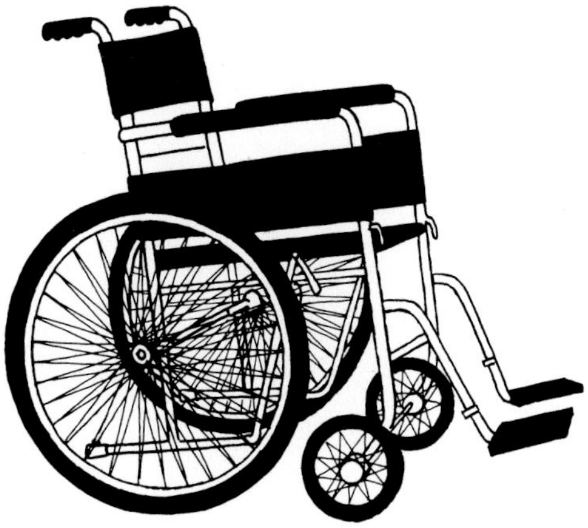

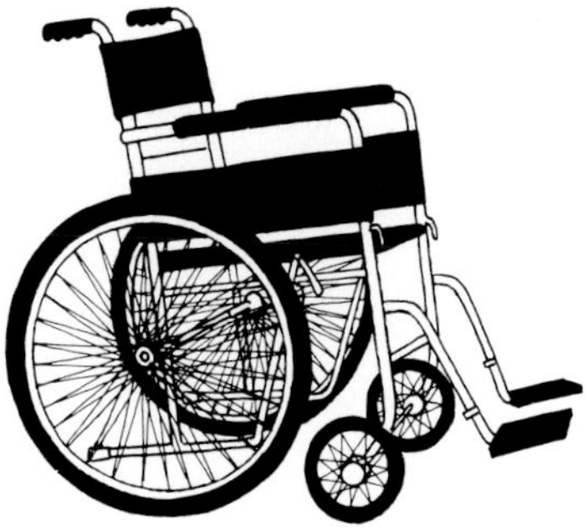

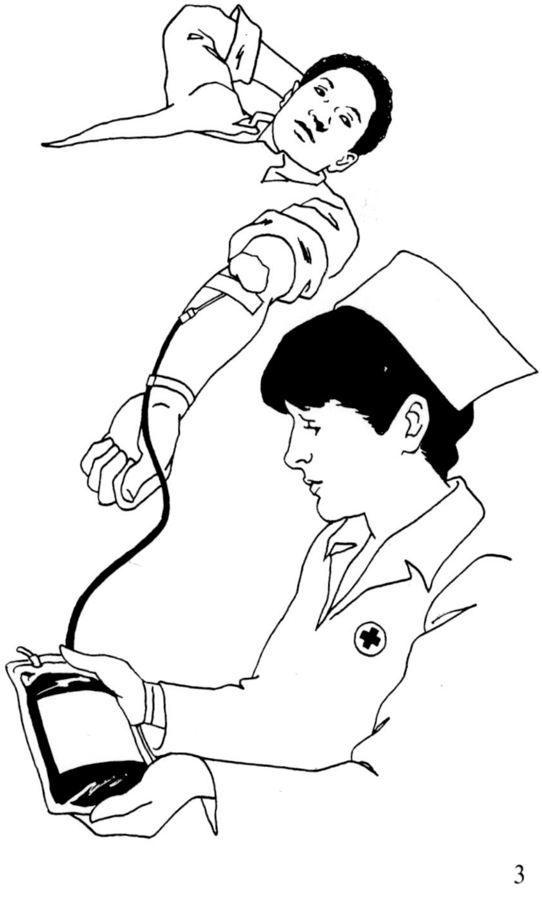

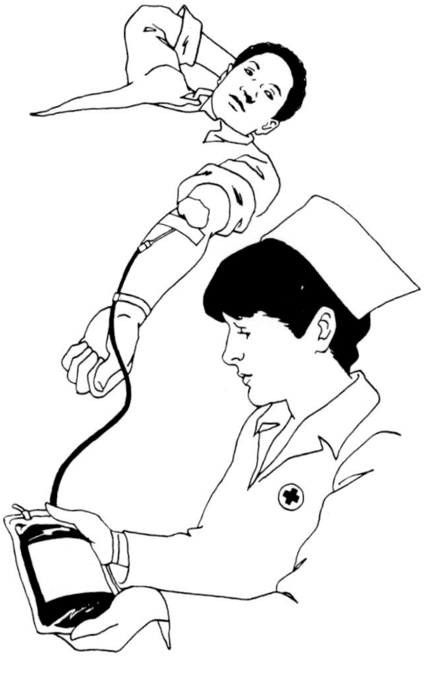

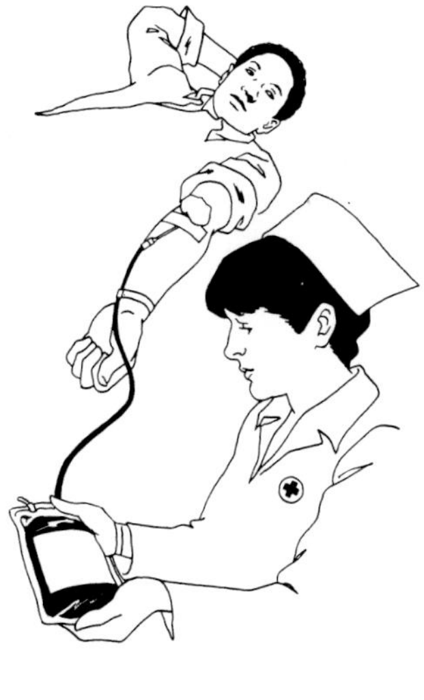

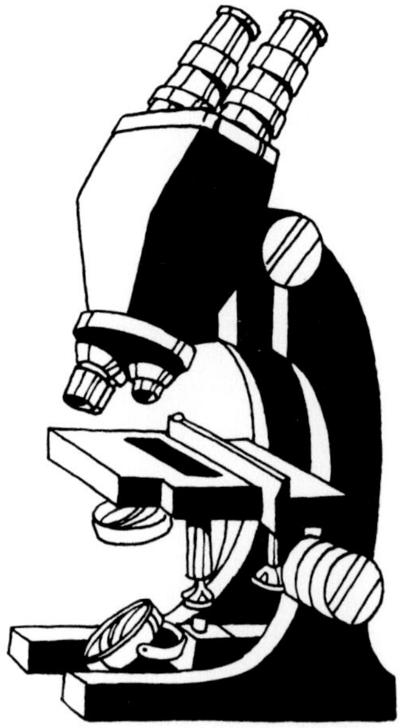

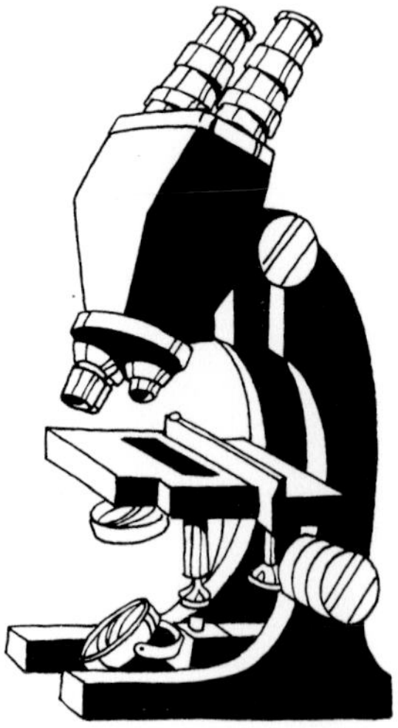

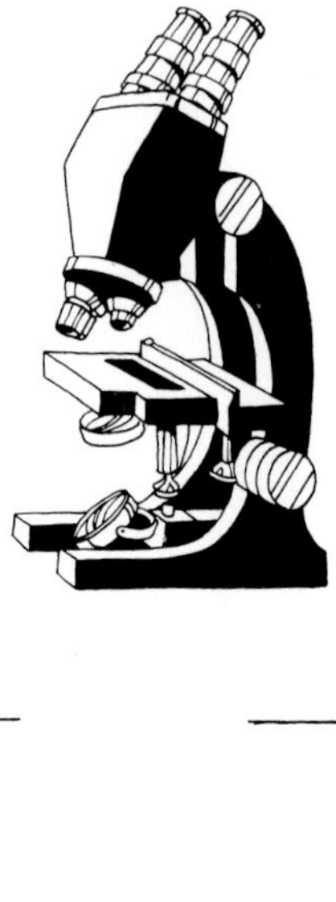

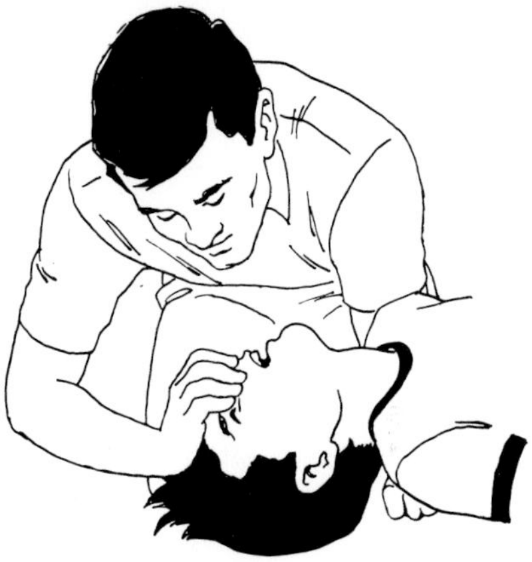
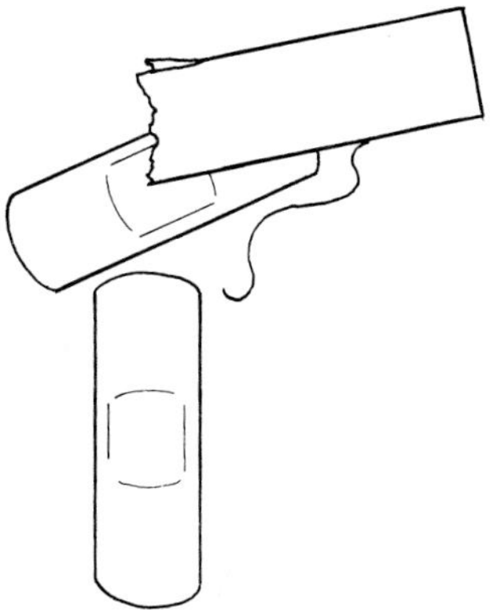

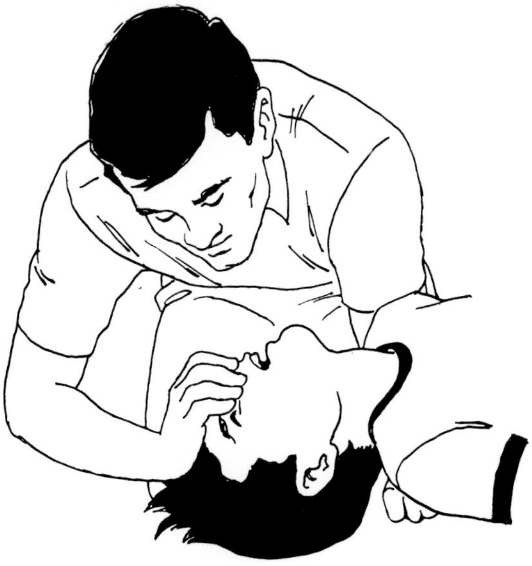
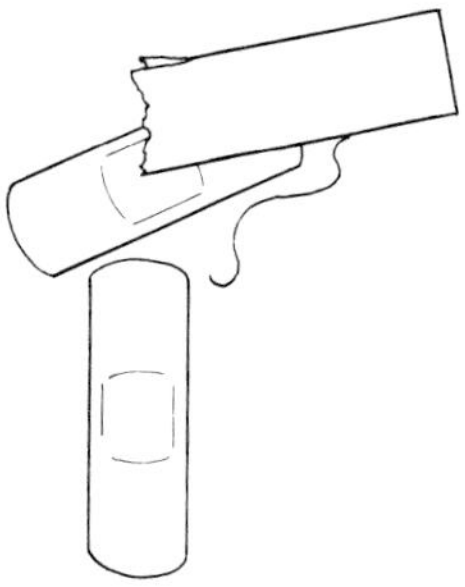

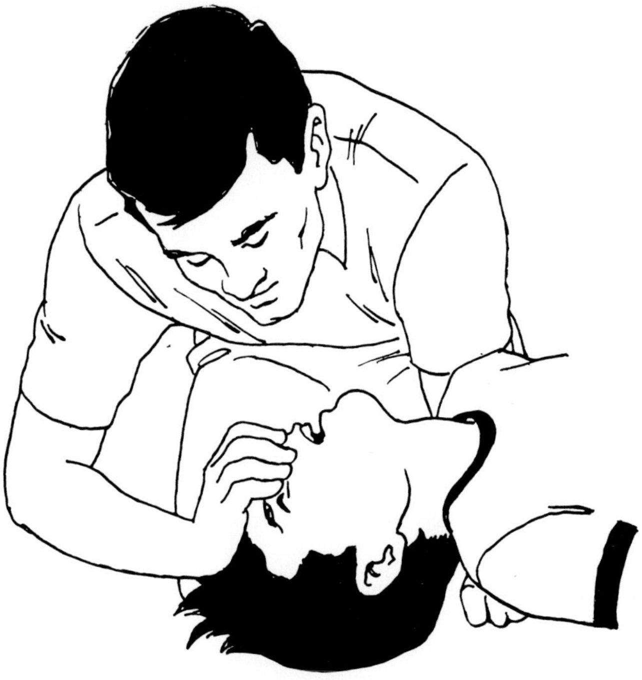
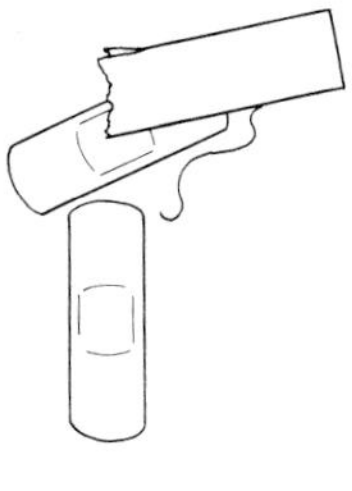

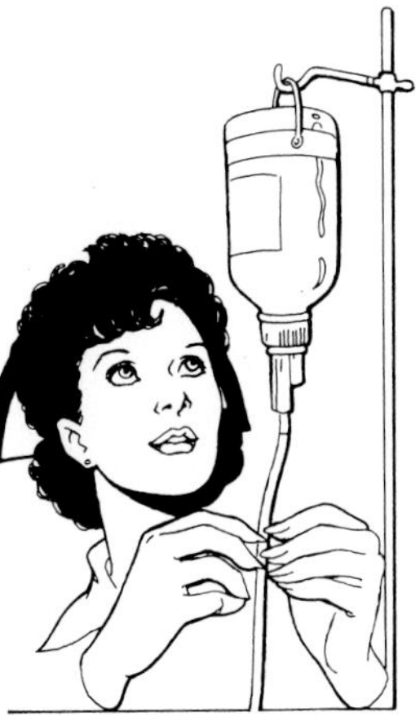
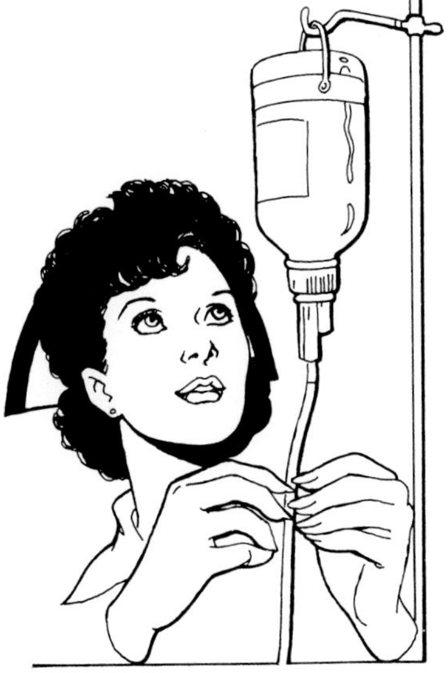
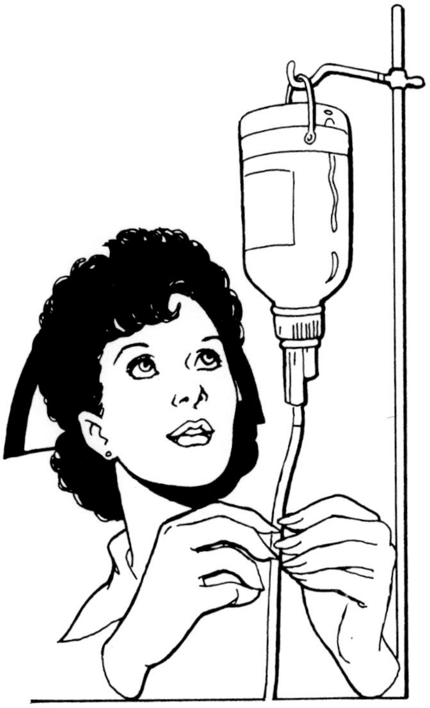

Rx

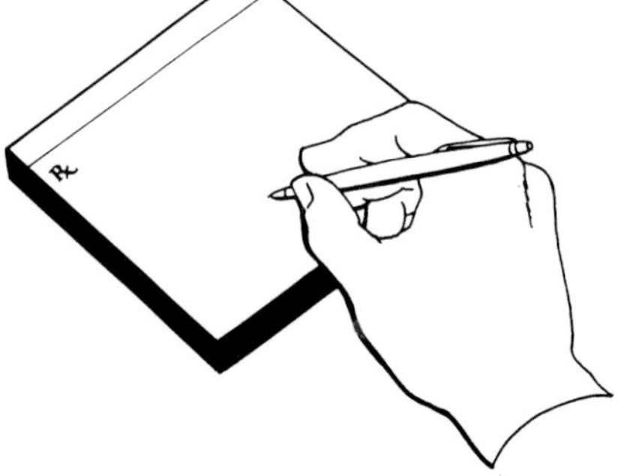
Rx

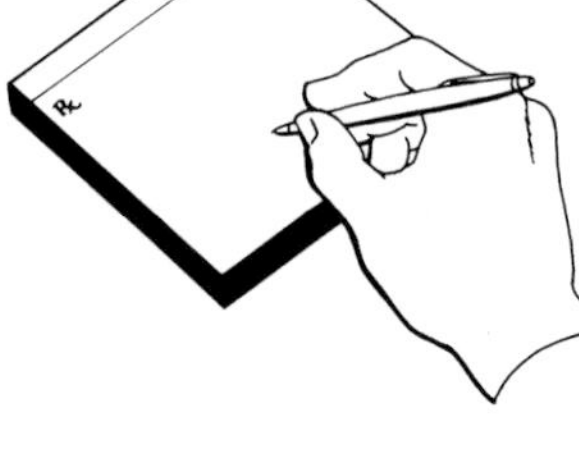
Rx

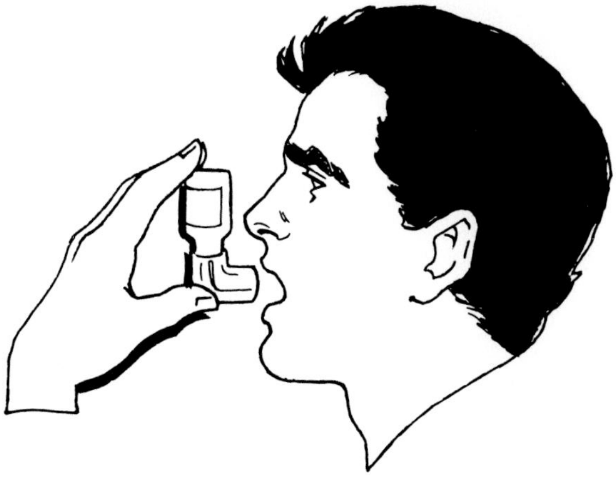

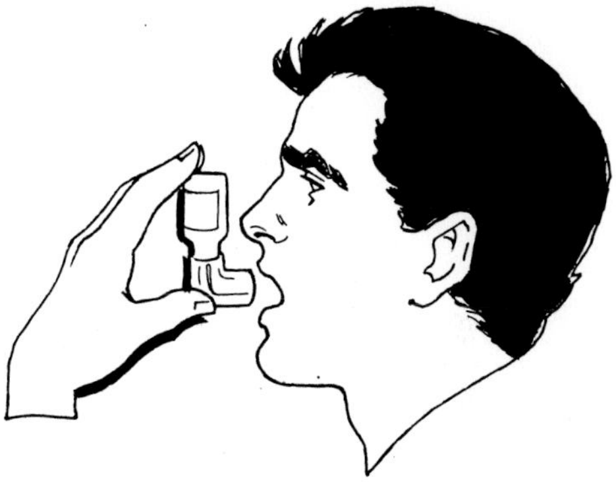

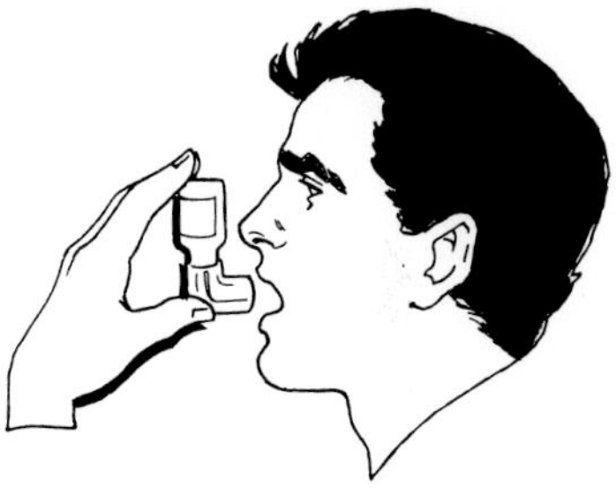

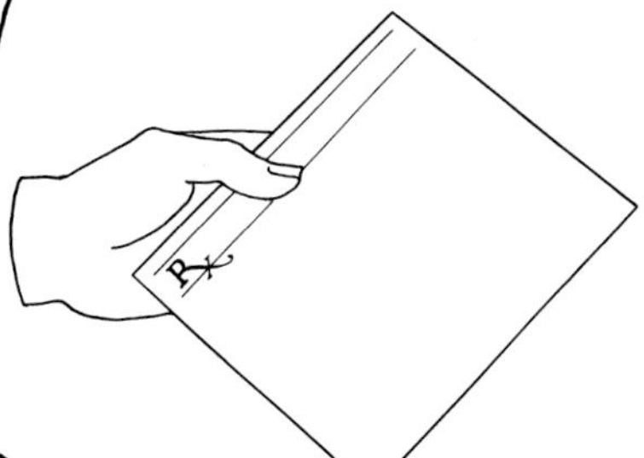

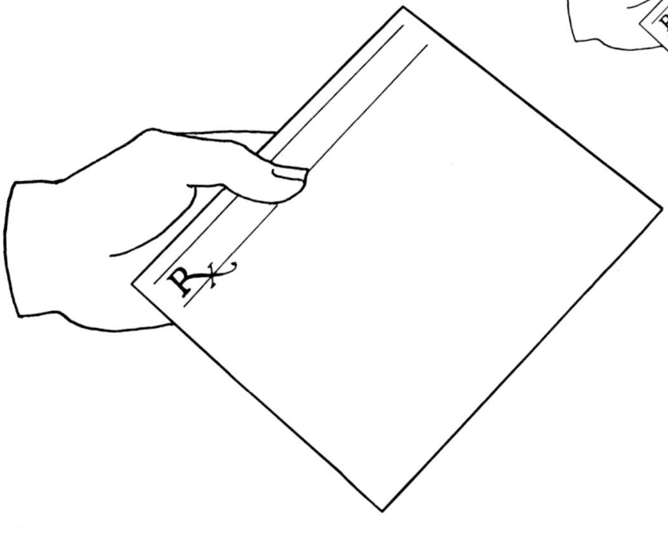

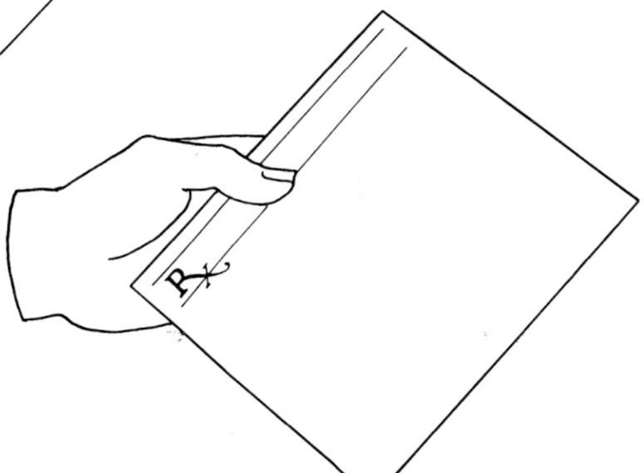

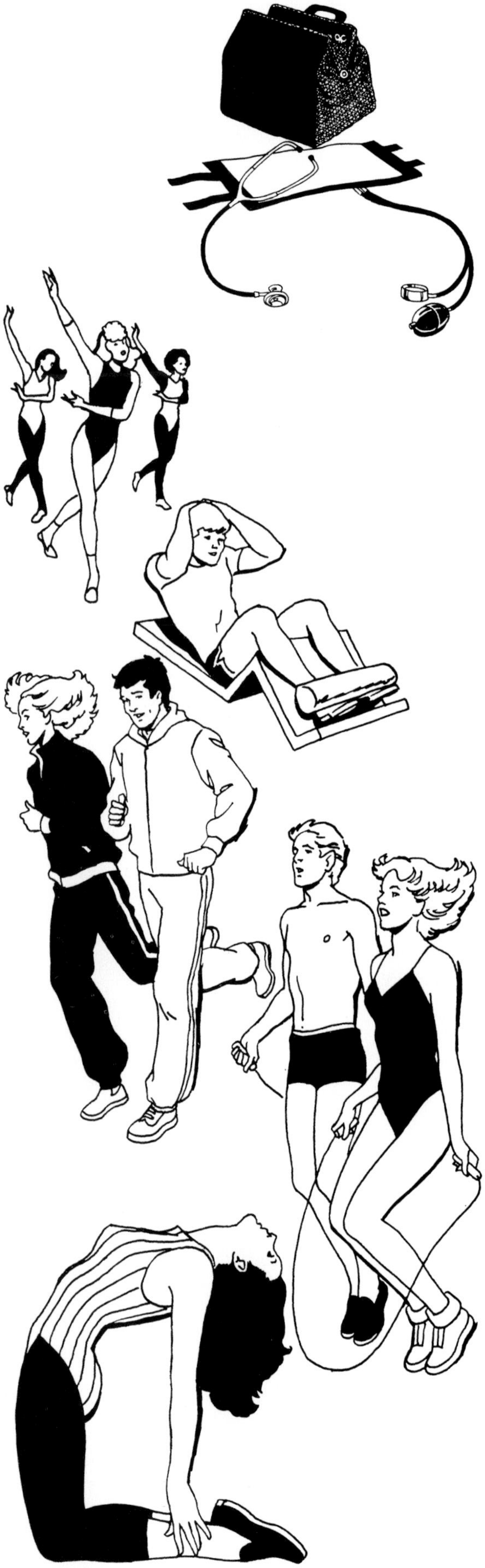

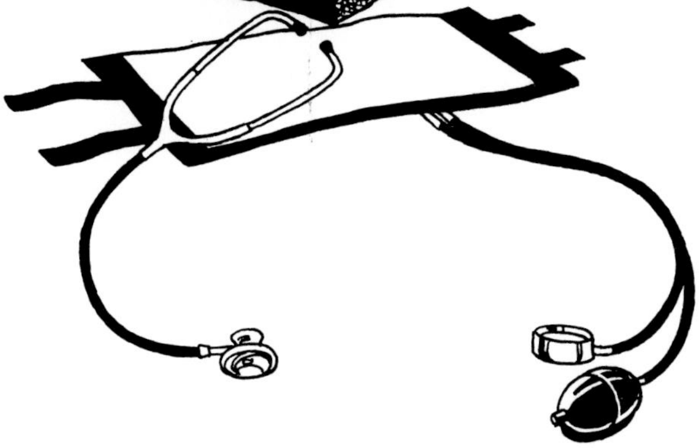

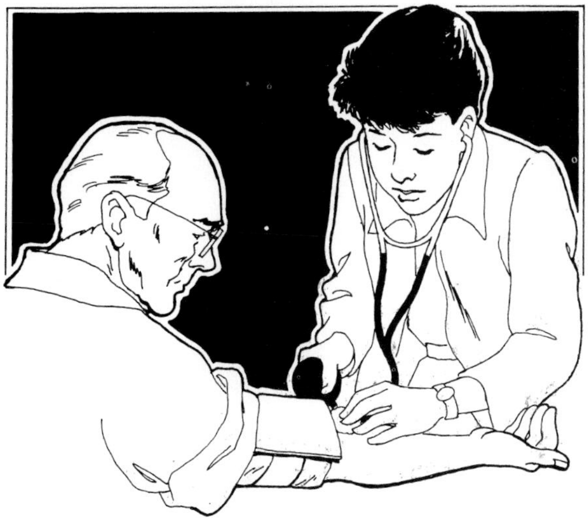

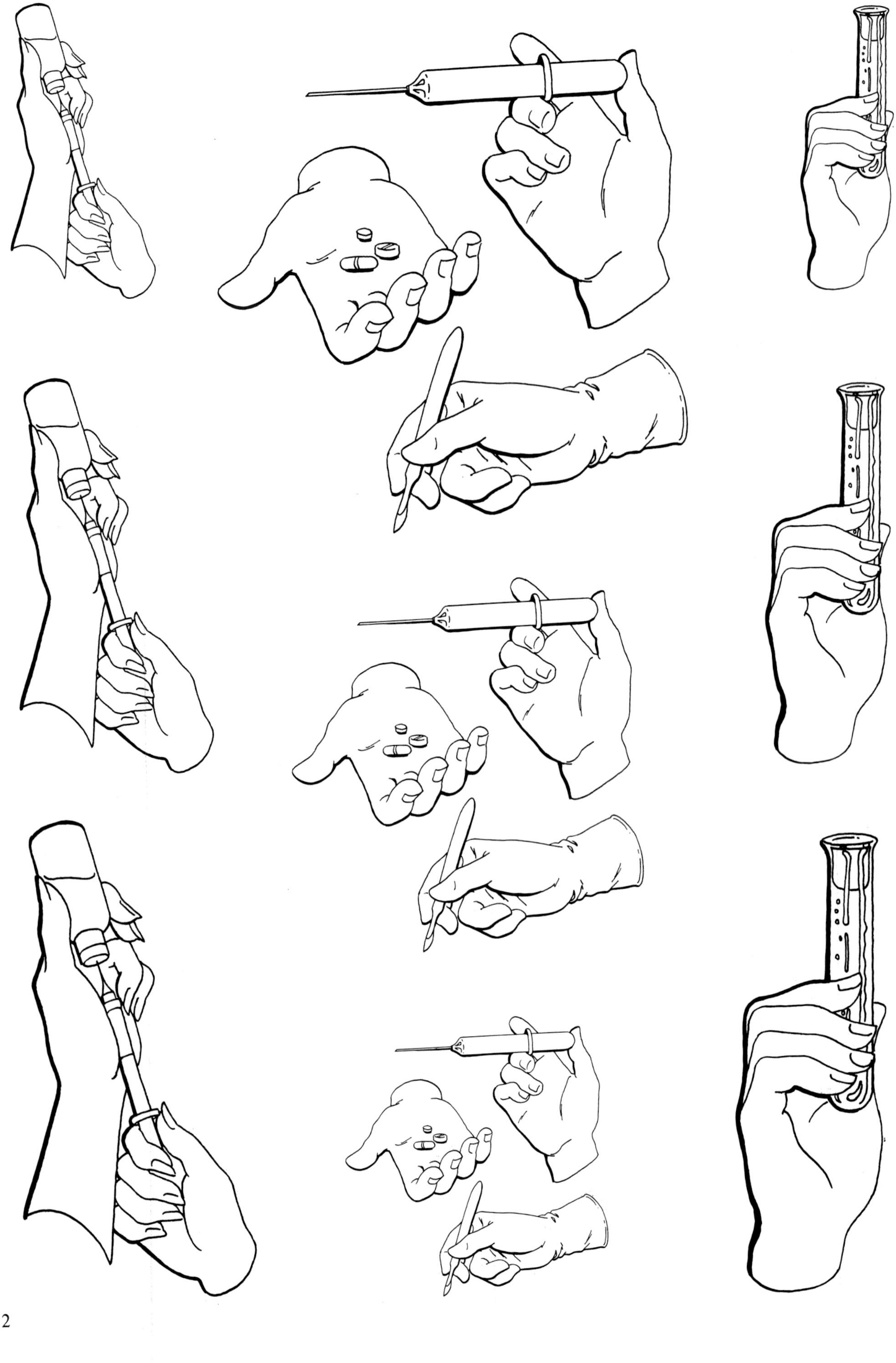

AMBULANCE

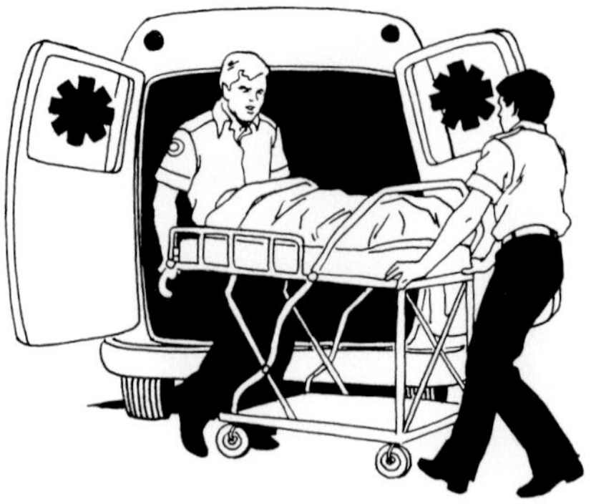

AMBULANCE

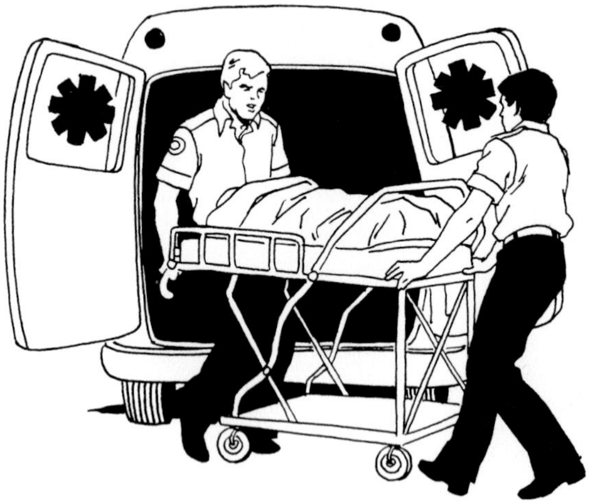

AMBULANCE

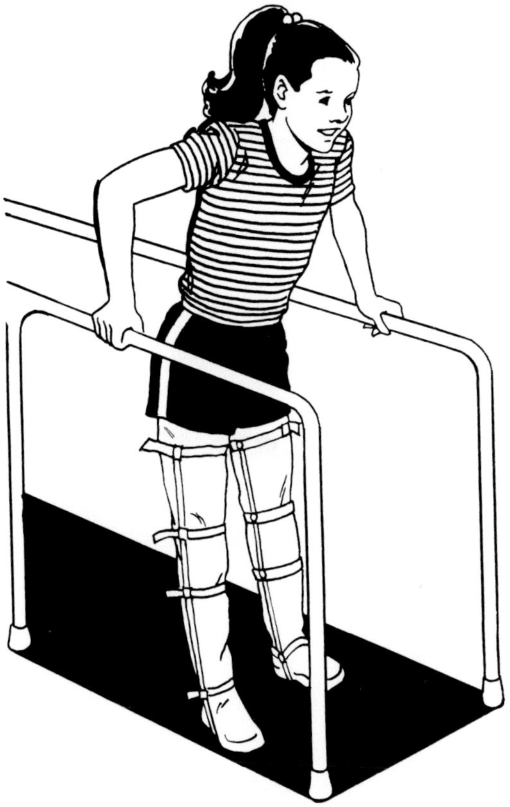
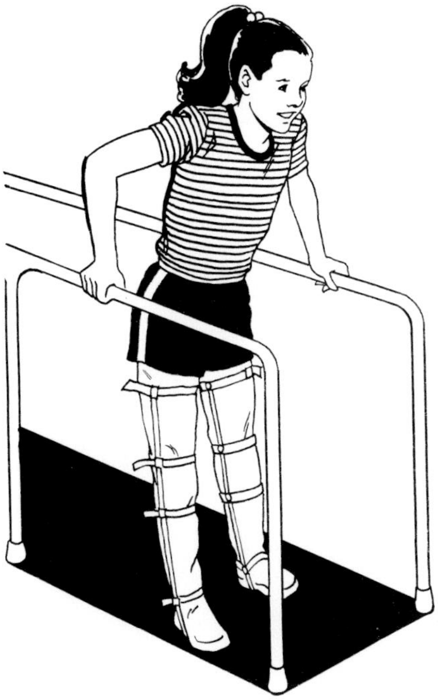
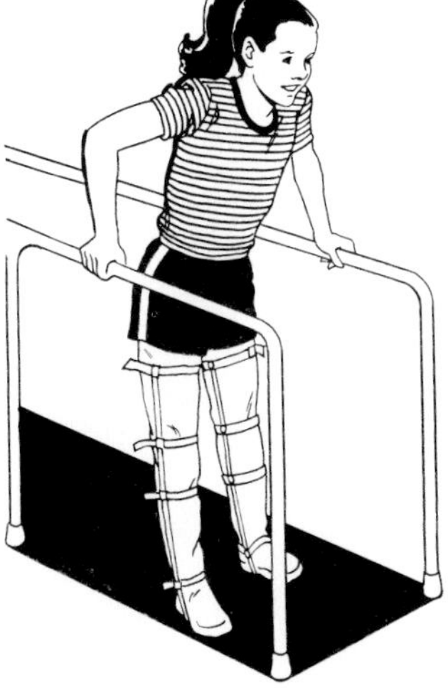

WAITING

WAITING

WAITING

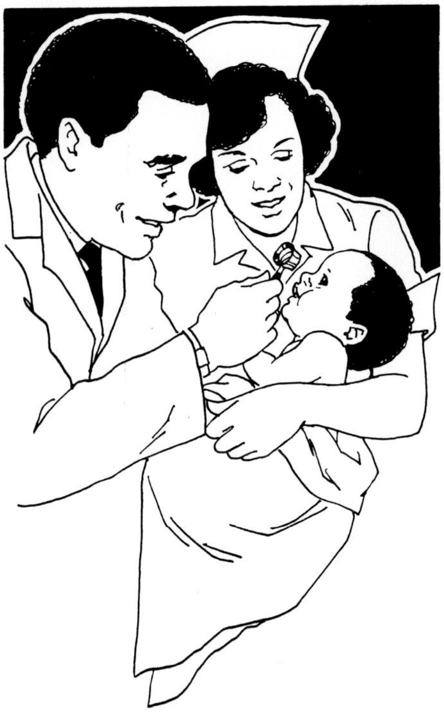

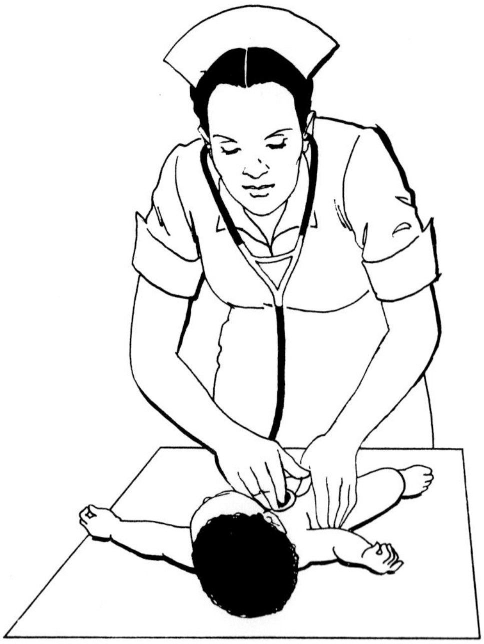
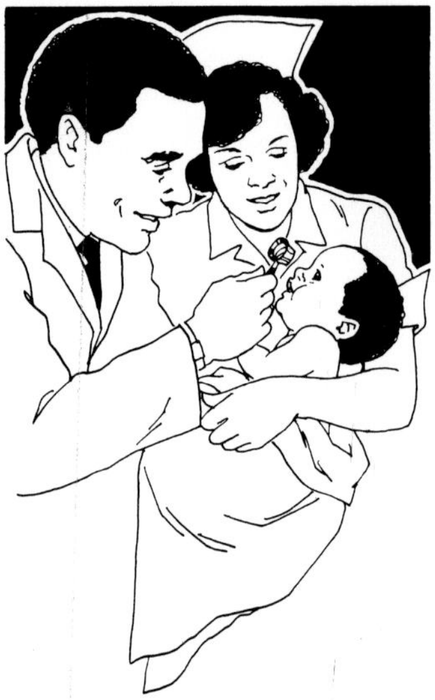

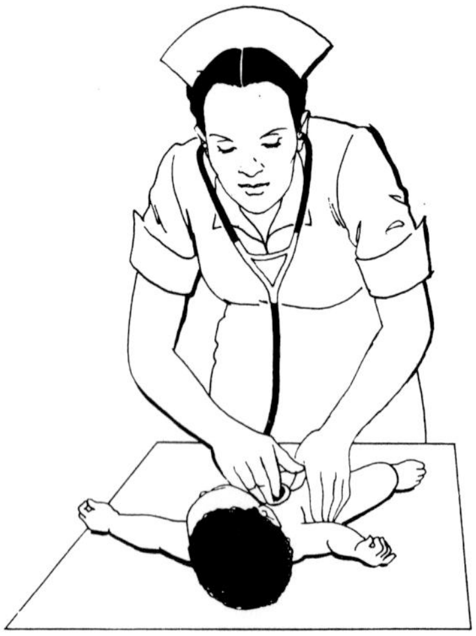

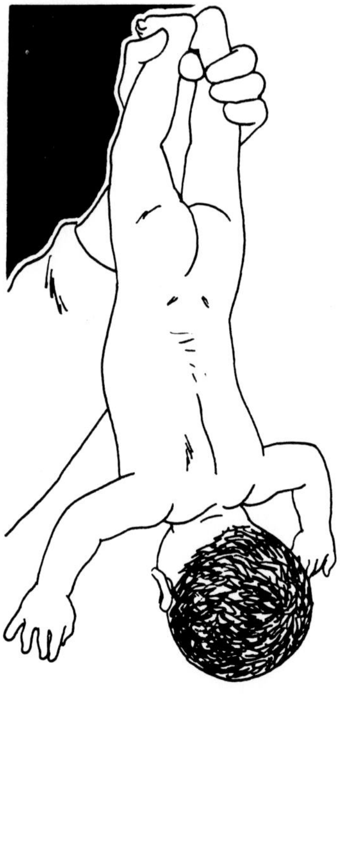
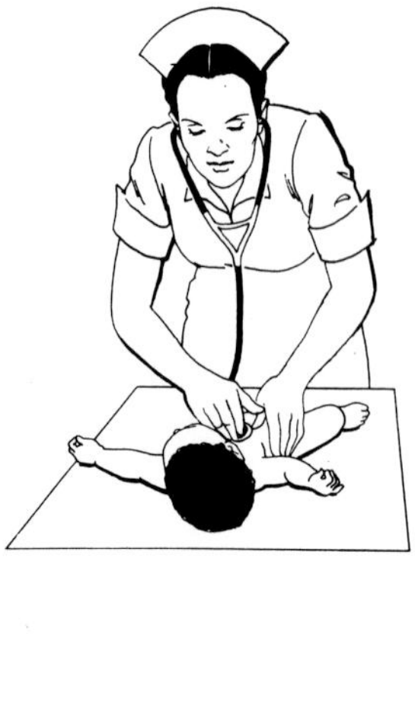

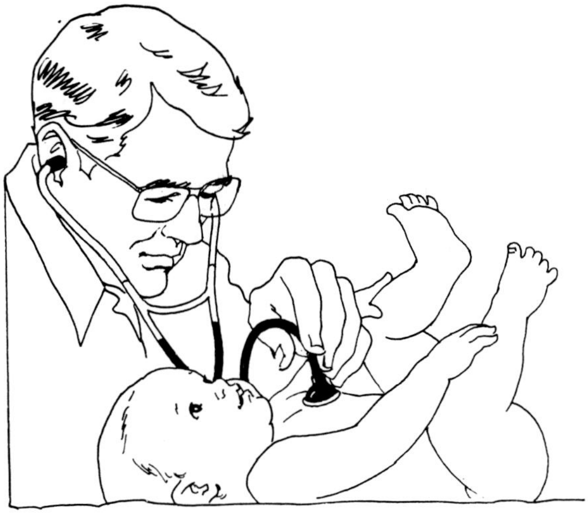
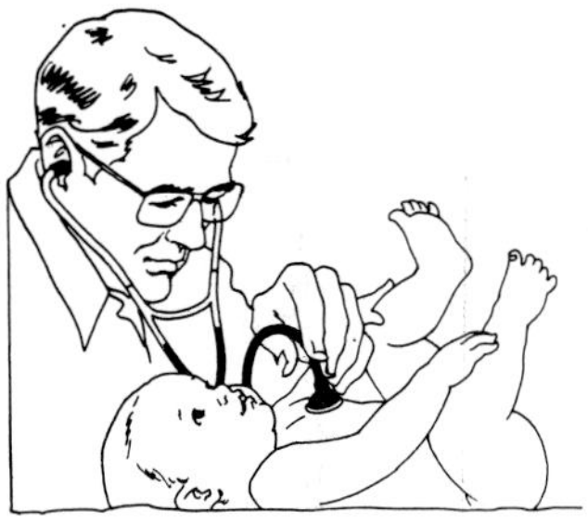
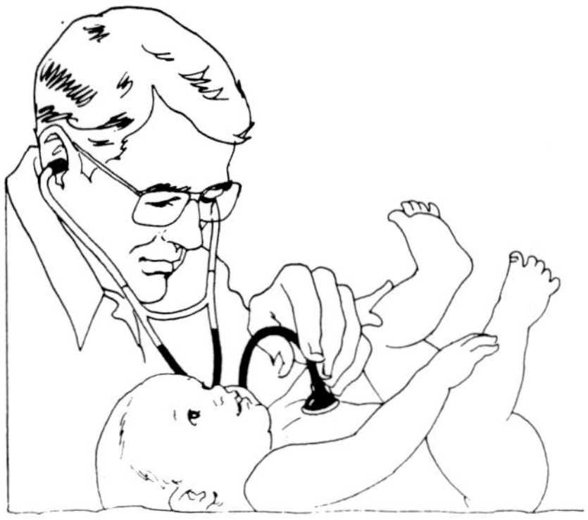
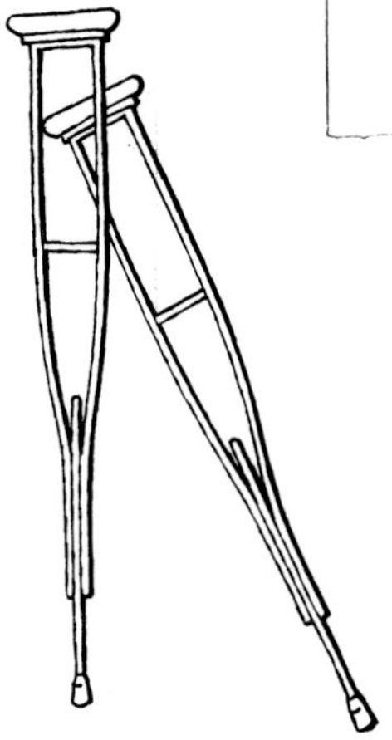

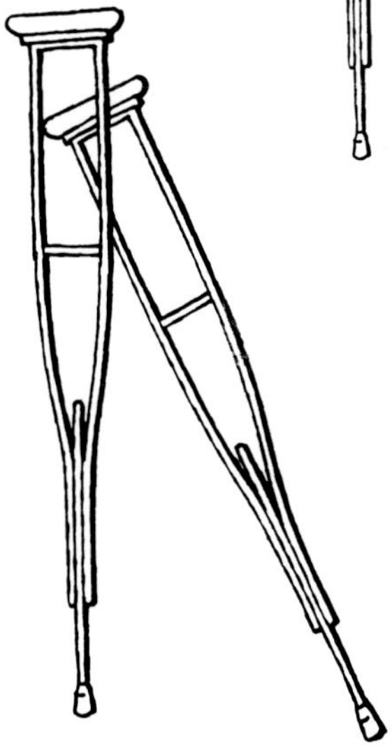

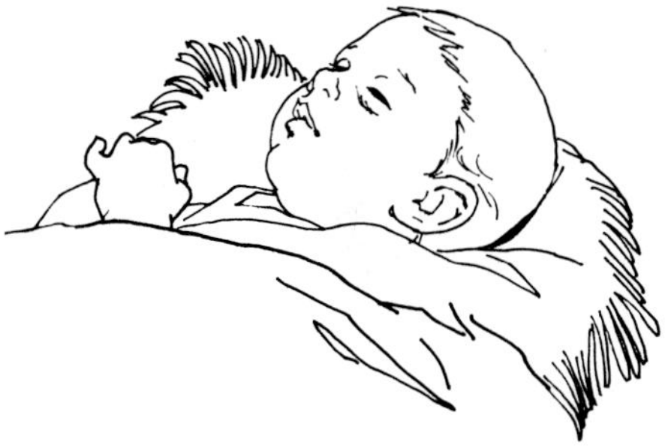
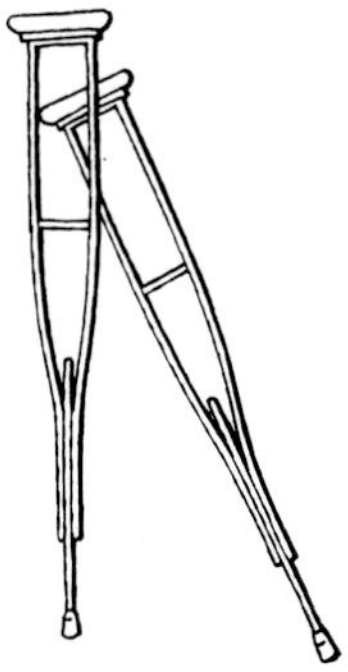

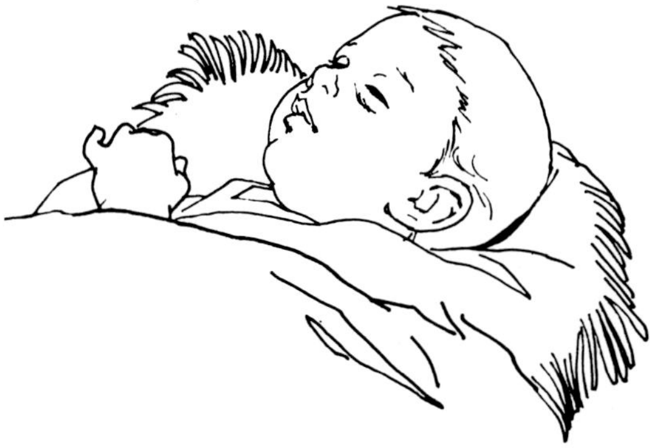

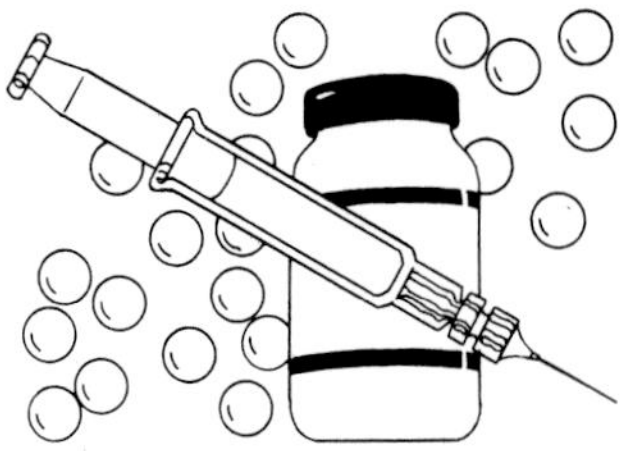

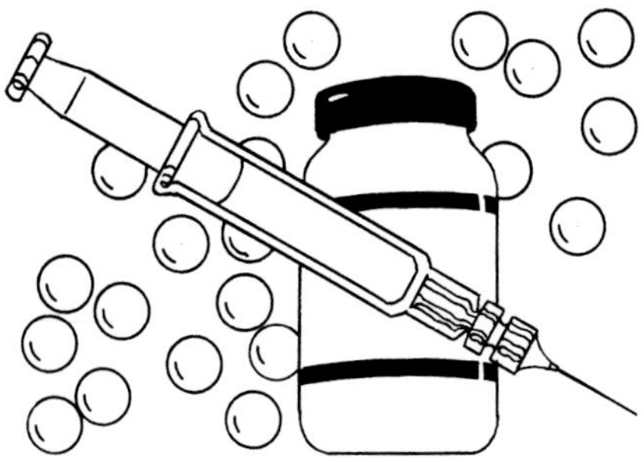

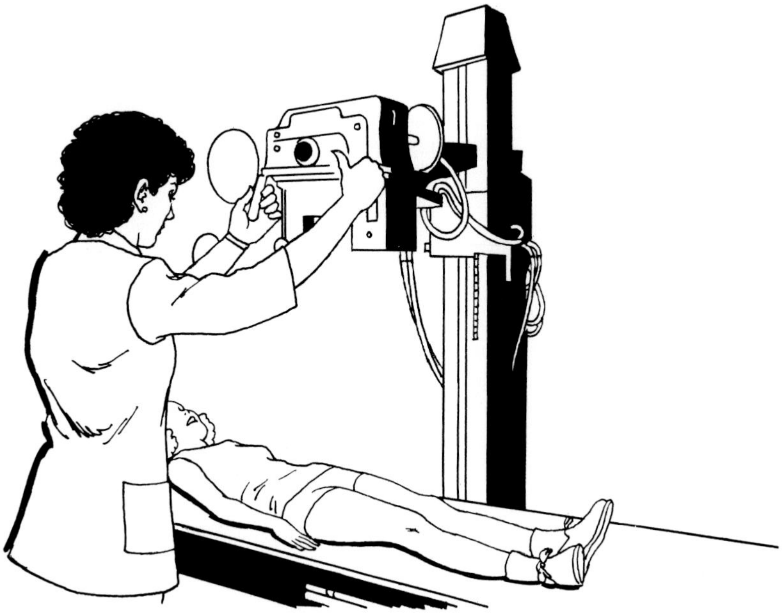

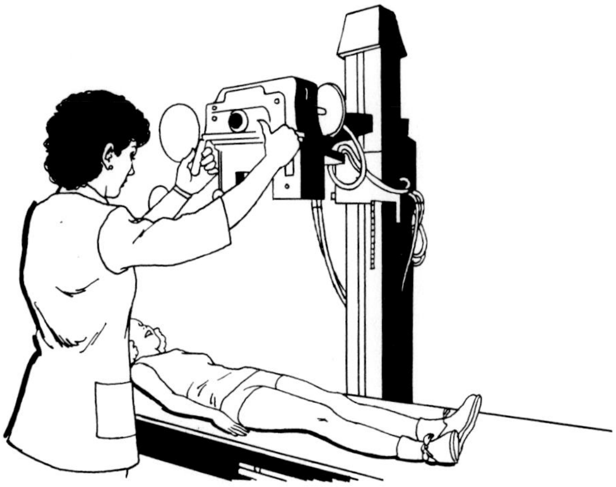

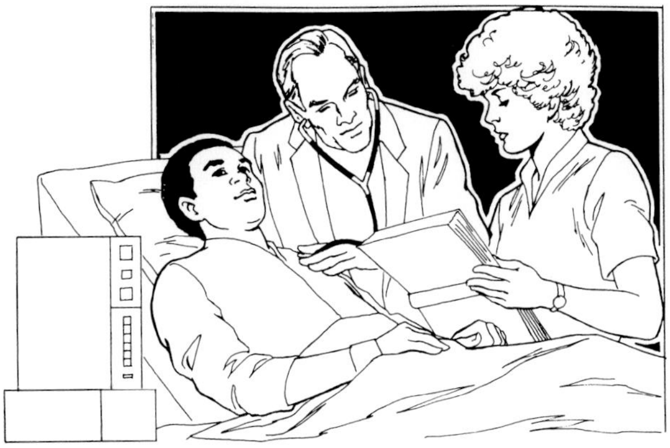

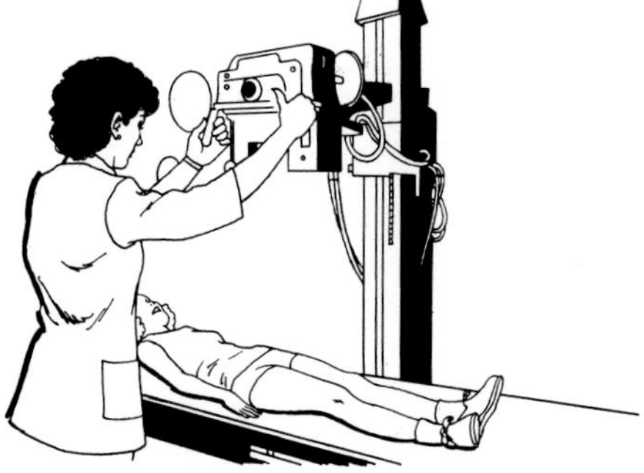

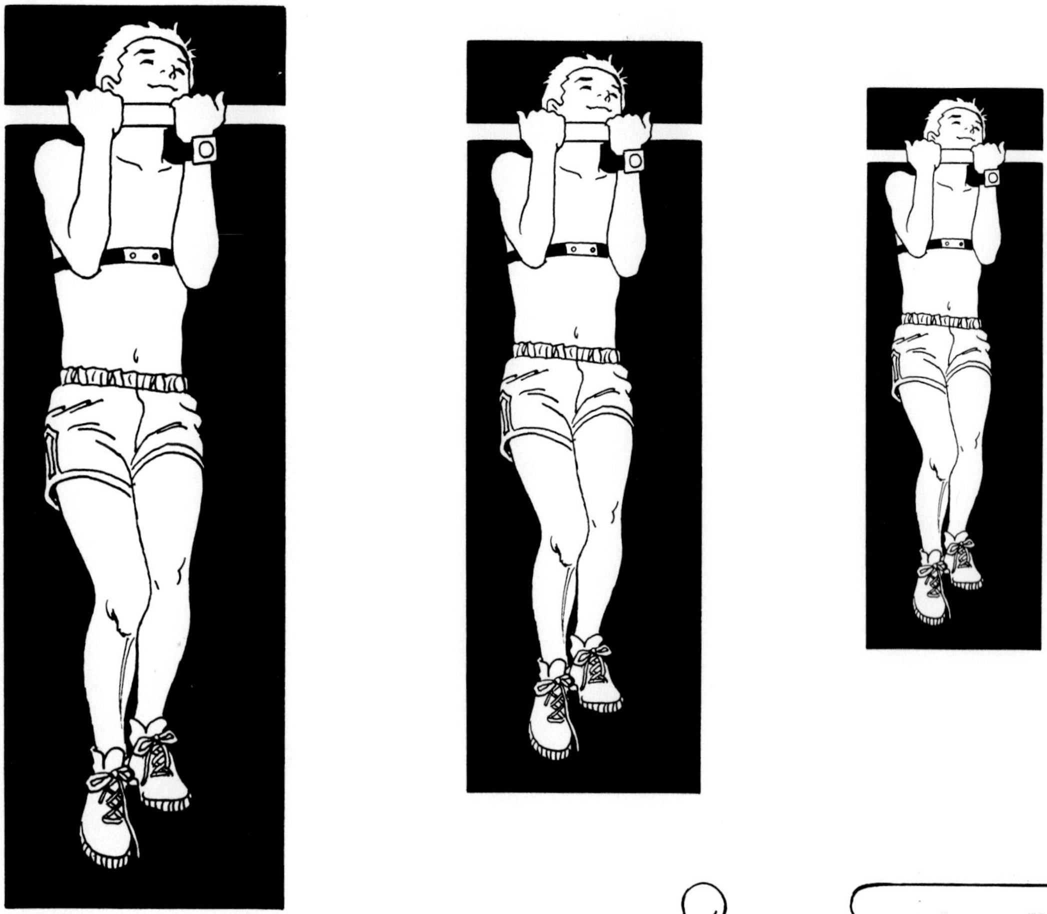

Rx
Rx
Rx

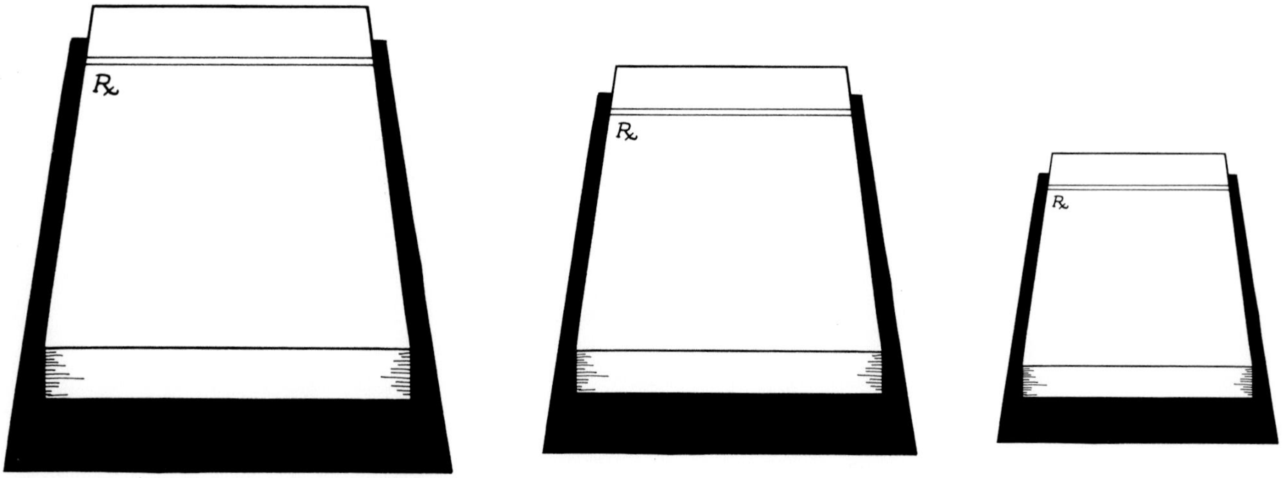
Rx
Rx
Rx

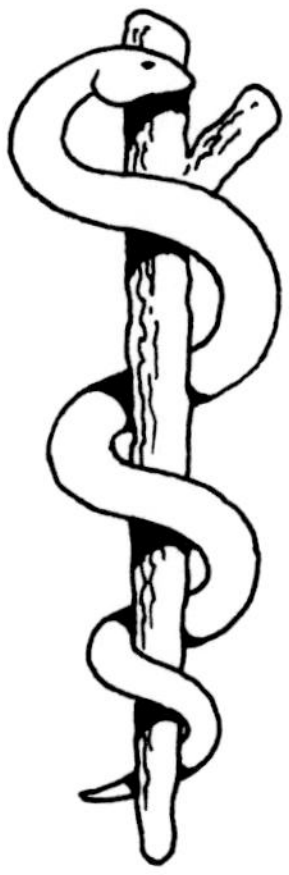

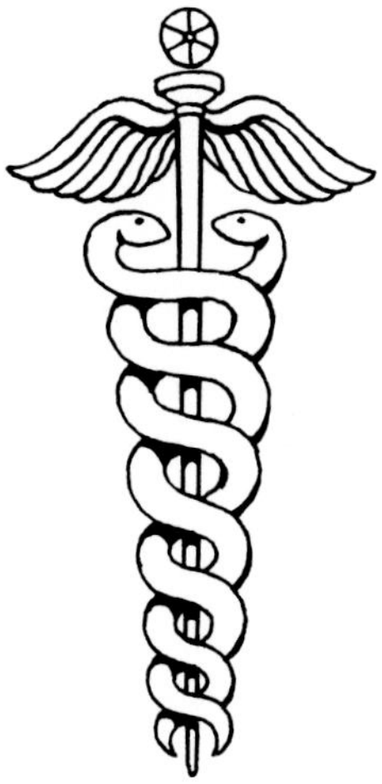

CRIPTIONS

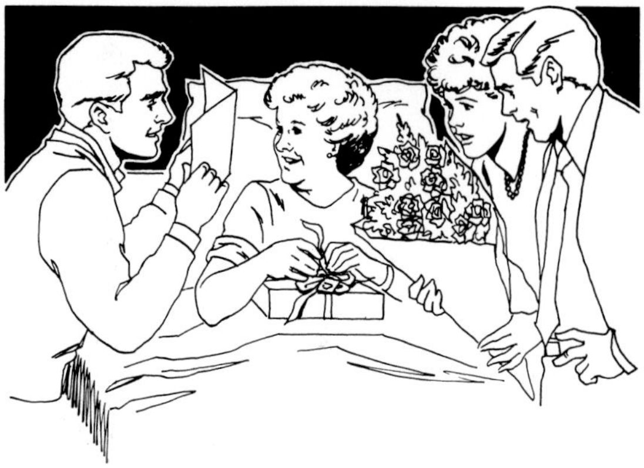

CRIPTIONS

CRIPTIONS

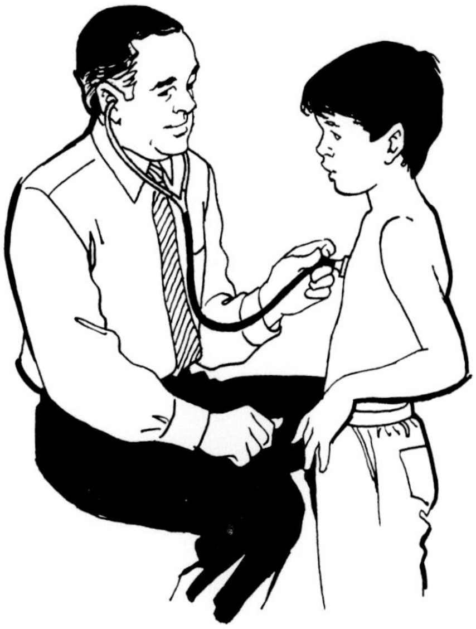

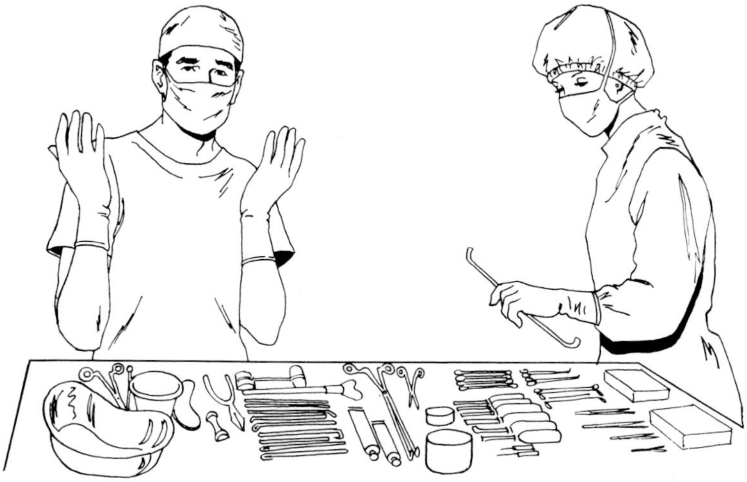

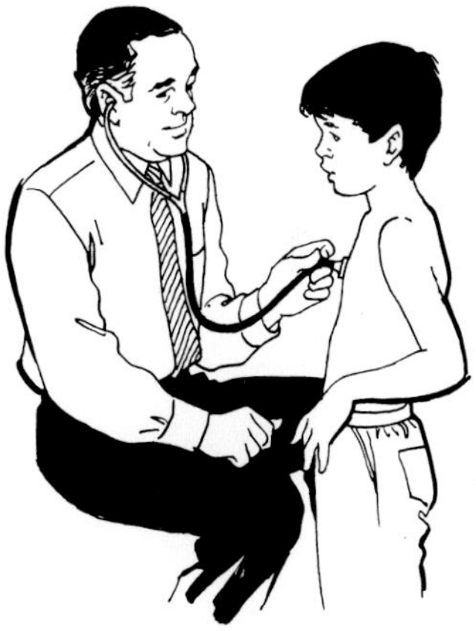

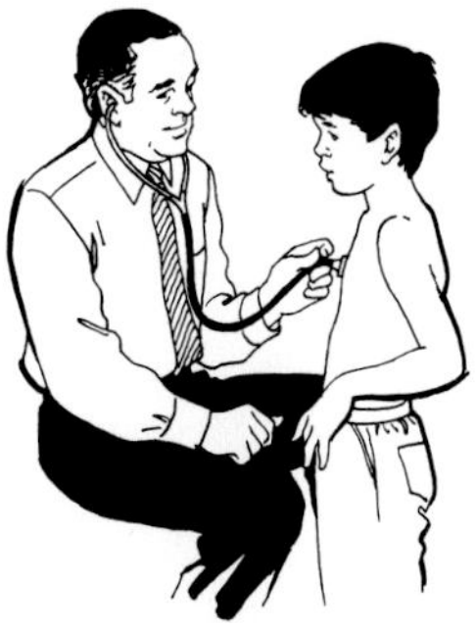

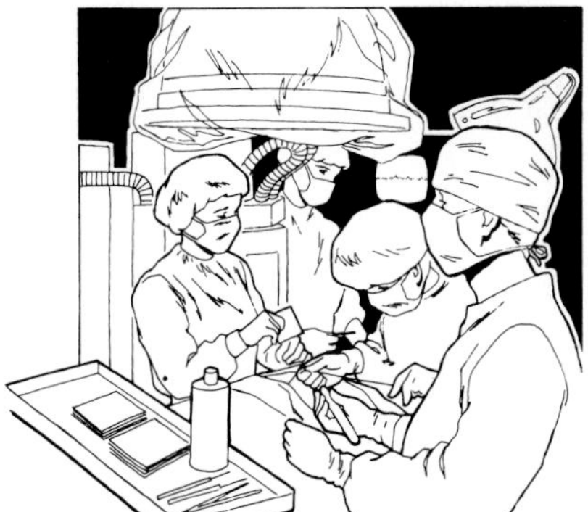

Rx

Rx

Rx
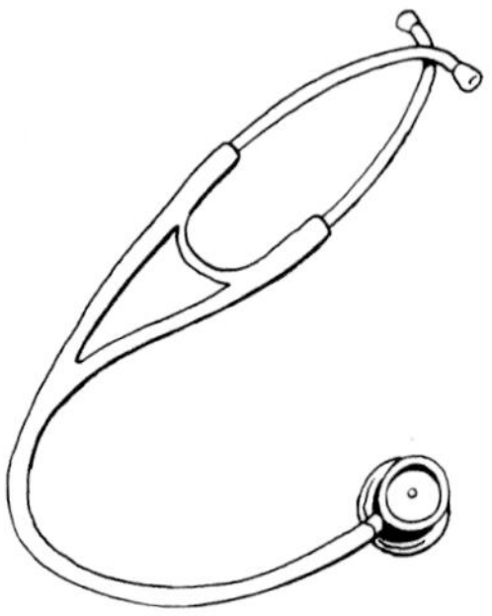
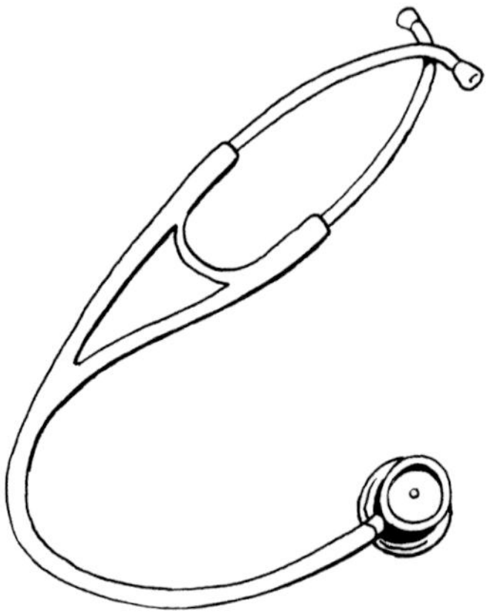
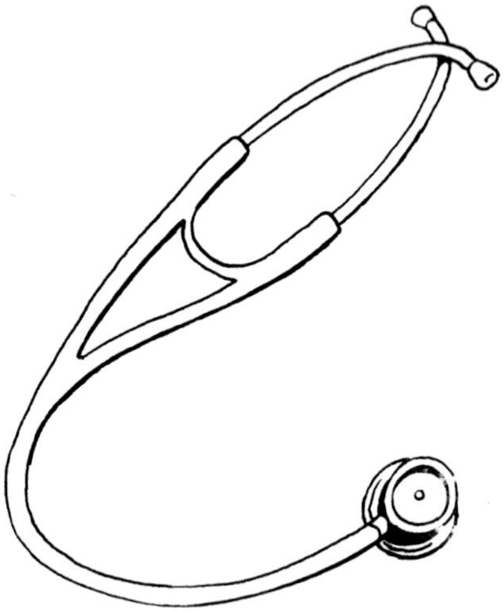

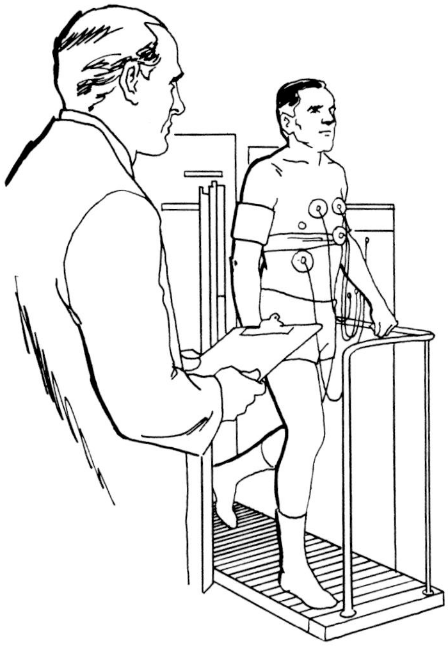

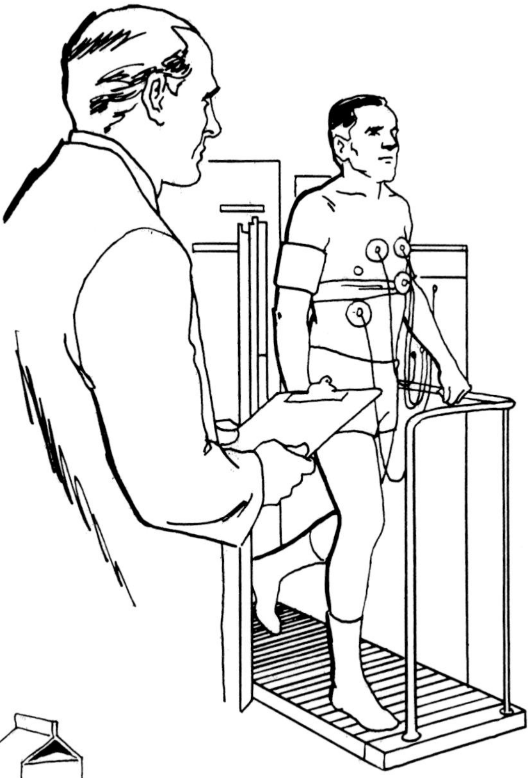

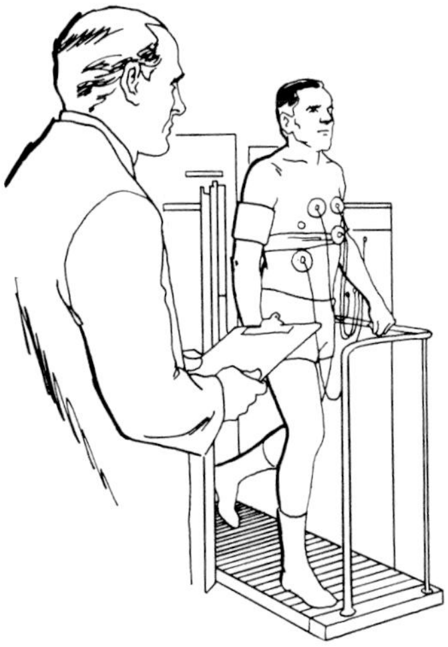

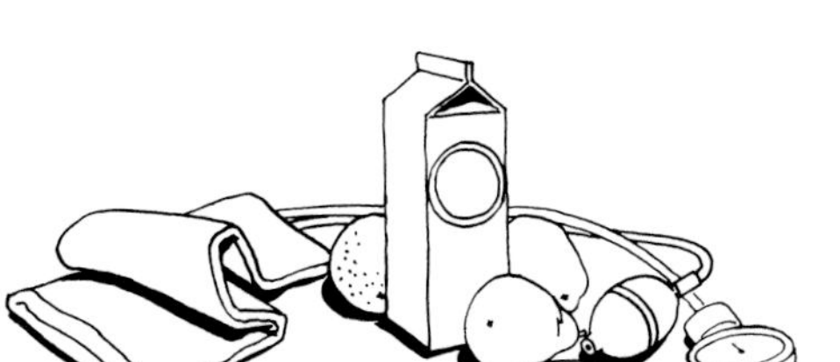

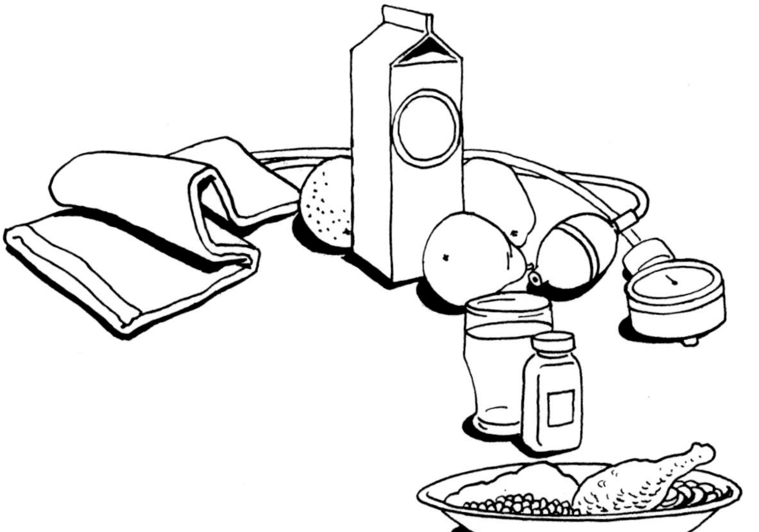

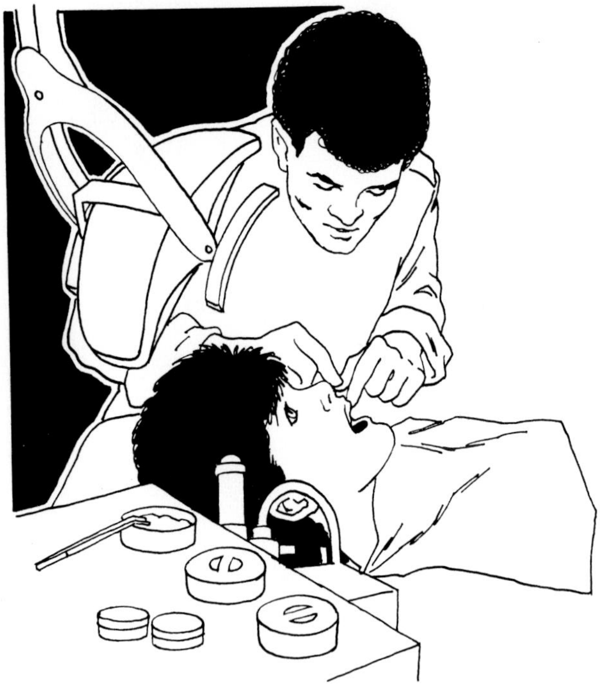

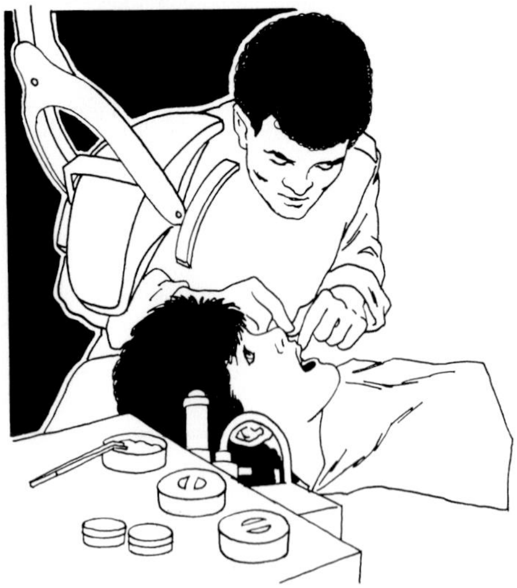

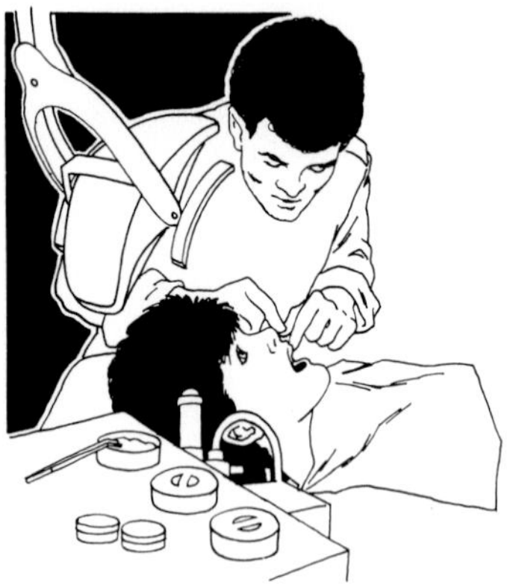

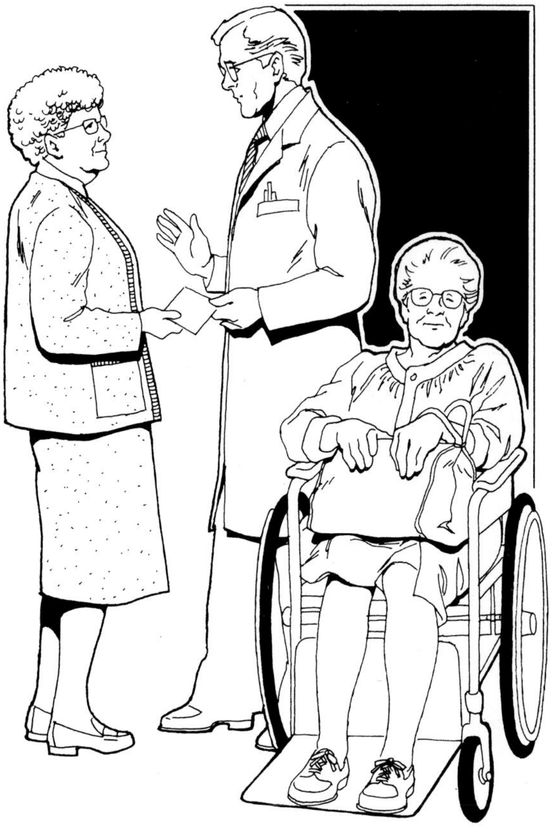

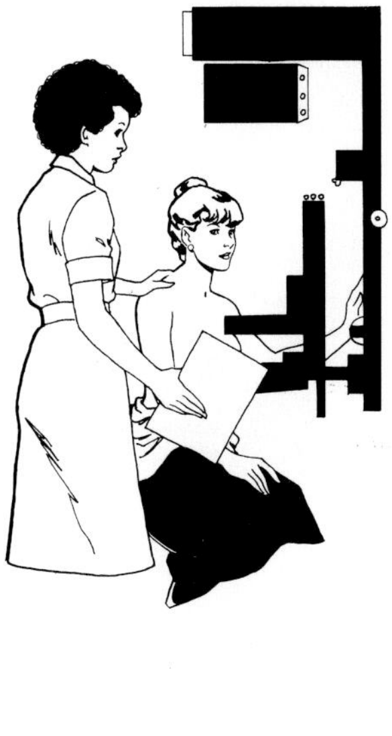

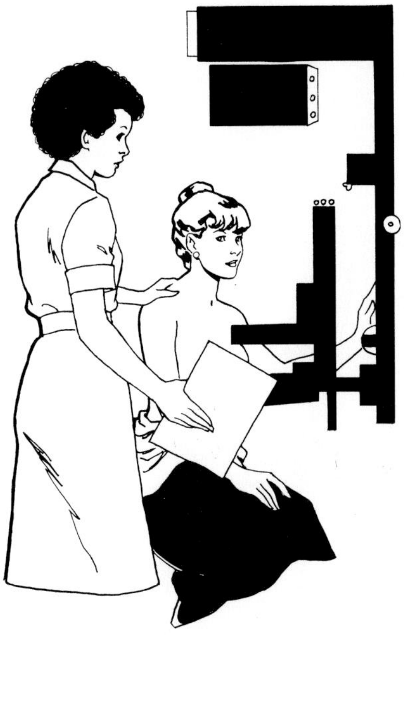

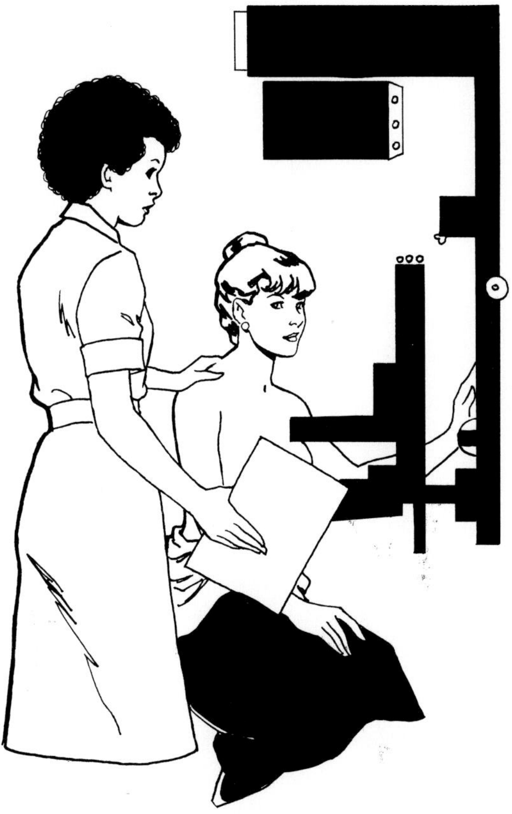

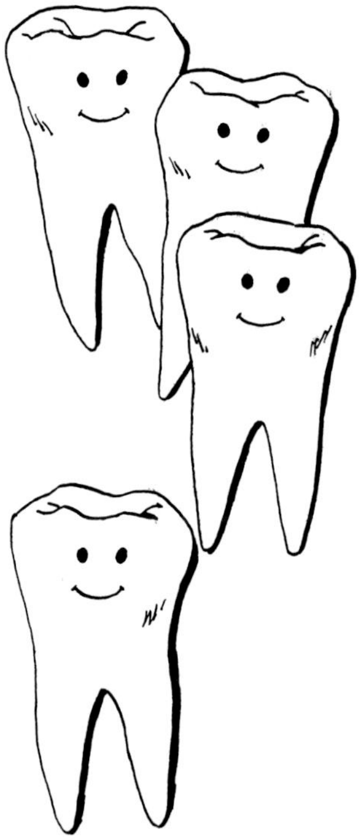
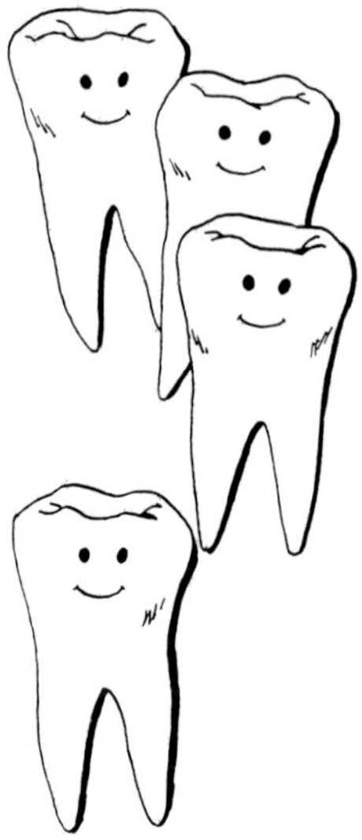

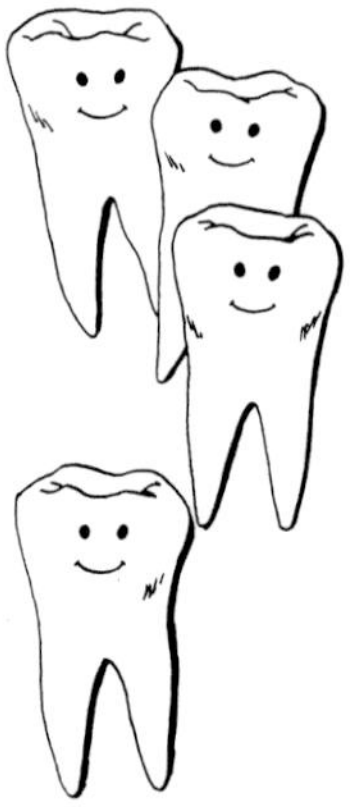

Rx
for Good Health

Rx
for Good Health

Rx
for Good Health